Extrovert Yourself

How to Become Extrovert, Confident and Overcome Shyness

Jack Daniels

Table of Contents

Introduction

"I want this." For a lot people, it is the easiest thing in the world to say. Life is pretty nice for these kinds of assertive and confident people. They usually end up with the window seat on airplanes, the last slice of pizza, and a cubicle that's not by the bathroom. However, not everybody is naturally confident and assertive, even if they are loud.

If you are the type of person who is introverted and shy, you may not be as comfortable talking about yourself. Saying what you want or what you think when you are around many people can be difficult. Fear not, however, for in this book, we will give you tips on how to become more assertive and confident. In addition to that, we will also teach how to conquer or overcome fear and how to deal with shyness, which tends to be the cause of many confidence issues.

So, without further ado, let us go ahead and take your first step into becoming a more confident and extroverted person.

Chapter 1 - An In-depth Understanding of Extroverts and Introverts

Before we begin to talk about ways on how to become extroverted, let us first talk about what is an introvert and an extrovert, and how does these two different types of personalities can affect your life. To fully grasp the techniques that we're going to discuss about how to extrovert yourself, we must not only be interested in just defining introversion and extroversion, but also on how to take these two and start to tune them to get the best results.

In this chapter, we are going to go into a deeper understanding of introversion versus extroversion. We are going to talk about the origins of these terms, their pros and cons, and the techniques on how to become extroverted at will. If you are looking forward to being more extroverted, then we have got you covered here.

Before we get into the more in-depth definition of extroversion and introversion, let's first talk a little bit about their history-- where did these terms even come from. The term "Extrovert" and "Introvert" came from a psychologist in the early 1900s named Carl Jung.

During that time, Carl Jung created different psychological archetypes with a particular focus on the common strands between people. Some of the archetypes that he identified are now used in the Myers-Briggs personality assessment, which you may have taken at work, school, online, and other similar places. From there, he made two fundamental distinctions in psychology: the introvert and the extrovert.

According to Jung, an introvert is someone who enjoys, and is more comfortable, being by himself. In a sense, introverts are in their head more than they are out in the real world. They are deep thinkers, they like to be alone, they don't particularly enjoy being in loud and noisy environments, and their energy tends to drain when they're out there socializing with other people.

An introvert is often stereotyped as a "shy" person. The extrovert, on the other hand, is the complete opposite of the introvert. The extrovert is the social butterfly - the person who loves to go out there and mingle with people. An extroverted person loves to talk, he likes to tell stories, he is verbose, he is really excited about meeting new people, he draws his energy from other people in his immediate vicinity, and he doesn't like to be by himself all the time. In other words, an extrovert is more sensory, rather than logical and analytical.

As far as deeply understanding what extroverts and introverts are, here is what is really going on. When people talk about the fact that an introvert's energy is drained when he is out talking to people, and how it is the opposite for an extrovert, it means that an introvert believes that his world is on his mind. He lives in a world of ideas. What is real is not out there. What is real is on his head.

In other words, he is so absorbed in the thoughts - the analysis and processing of all the sensory perception that he is getting from the world. Here is an example: When an extrovert goes in and he talks to a group of people, he will just go in there and immediately have something to say. In addition, he will also have enough energy to keep things going. When you ask an extrovert a question, he will just respond right off the bat.

Introverts, on the other hand, process the world differently. If someone asks an introvert a question, it takes him a second or two to process it and come up with an appropriate response. Introverts do not respond right off the bat.

The reason for this is because they are living in their own heads. Their reality is in the mind, not out in the world. It takes introverts more time and energy to process a question then give back a more appropriate and solid response. Also, while they're trying to come up with a response, they're also trying to see in their mind whether the response that they give is going to be accurate.

For introverts, value does not only fall on the response that they give. They also give value on how their response will be perceived, and how the person on the other end of their response will reply. In a way, we can say that introverts are more reflective. If an introvert says something, he is probably wondering how his statement will be received even before the person on the other side of the conversation actually says something.

For extroverts, however, the real world is out there. Their world is something that they can see, grope, smell, taste, hear, smile at, frown, have an emotional reaction with, and so forth.

Their thoughts about their world are only secondary. This does not mean that extroverts do not have any thoughts about anything. It is just that their thoughts are on an extremely fundamental level that they become just a secondary layer that is added later on.

Extroverts are not overly conscious about how they will be perceived by the people around them. Sometimes, they will say things that they don't even mean to say. This is especially noticeable when they are backtracking. Backtracking is when they say something wrong accidentally, quickly take it back then shift to a different topic. They will just gloss over the conversation and say something new.

The way it works for extroverts is that they have to say something first before they recognize whether it is real or not. They are just going to blurt it out there. They will not say it in their minds first the way introverts do. They will just blurt it out then think about how people will react later. This is the main reason why extroverts are more verbose and talkative.

Many times, extroverts seem shallower because they just throw stuff out there without thinking about it too much. This is what makes them so spontaneous, engaging and charismatic. This is where the extroverts and introverts differ - their perception of the world.

Pros and Cons

Now, let us talk a little bit about the pros and cons of introverts and extroverts. For starters, introverts are better at introspection. They can function better in those areas where analysis and logic are essential. They are experts at planning and are creative. An extrovert, on the other hand, functions better when socializing with people and doing things that require cooperation, management, leadership, and so forth.

The aforementioned are mostly on the surface level; we are painting broad strokes here. It does not mean that if you are extroverted, you cannot be a great writer or thinker. ON the other hand, if you are introverted, it does not necessarily mean that you cannot be a great manager or leader. You can.

There is, however, a trap where many people who belong to either of the two personalities, fall into. It is the trap of having an either-or mentality. Many people think that they have to be either an introvert, or an extrovert. The truth is, you do not have to choose sides. In fact, a well-rounded, fully self-developed person should be both.

You need to blend the two in one way or another. Combining both personalities allows you to get the best out of being an extrovert and introvert and making them your strengths. You can also drop the negative attributes of each personality. What is even greater is you will get conscious control over it.

Therefore, what does being in conscious control mean? Well, it means that when you need to be extroverted, for instance, you can go out there and be one at will. This is important because if you are introverted, for example, and you want to get that amazing result that you want in your life either success in business- or relationships - you really have get out a bit more and become extroverted. You have to do that work because if not, you can't make the most out of your life.

Therefore, we challenge you not to make it an either-or choice. You want to have both. You want to be a well-rounded person. With that in mind, in the next chapter, we will go through some practical techniques or specific ways that you can go about starting to change yourself for the better.

Chapter 2 - Beginning your Transition to Extroversion

Now that we have discussed what really goes on in an introvert and extrovert's mind, the next thing we must talk about is how to transition from being introverted to being extroverted effectively. Just like what we mentioned in the previous chapter, to further your potential as a well-rounded person, you have to blend extroversion with introversion.

Before we proceed, if you are still unsure whether you are introverted, then go ahead and take the Myers-Briggs personality assessment. You can find that online and either pay a small price for it, or take it for free. There are many personality assessments out there. However, Myers-Briggs is considered as the best. Take the assessment and see where it places you.

After discovering that you are indeed an introvert and you decide you want to make some changes because you noticed that being too much of an introvert is negatively affecting some parts of your life, then what you want to do is follow the techniques that we will discuss.

So, if you are extremely introverted and you want to become more extroverted, here are some ways to do it:

Tip #1 - Start Going to Bars and Clubs

While this may look drastic for some, it is actually not. To begin your transition to extroversion, what you need to do is to go out there and start interacting with people. Get into really sociable environments where people are free to talk.

Bars and clubs are great because people tend to display their crazy and carefree personality there. Being there presents you with a challenge to talk to people. At first, you are going to feel extremely uncomfortable. However, as you spend more time there, your shell is going to open up and you are going to get more comfortable, which is exactly what you need.

We would also like to encourage you to do all of these without taking a drink. Drinking does indeed take away any inhibitions that you have. However, this is more of an artificial approach and does not really help you to become extroverted in the long run. Try to socialize in bars and clubs without drinking and see how that feels. It's going to feel really challenging and scary at first, but you can expect to achieve growth here in terms of socializing.

Tip #2: Try to Join Social Groups

Try to look for groups of like-minded people whom you can interact with. They can be religious groups, meet-up groups, or any group of people who are into whatever it is that you are interested in.

You can also go online and look for different groups from there. When we say online, we do not mean you form groups that hang out in virtual chat rooms or forums. What we mean is try to form real-life, face-to-face groups through online correspondence. You can never develop some extroverted traits through an online chat forum or over Skype. The only real way to build extroversion is through face-to-face interaction with other people.

Tip #3: Be More Talkative

Stop being so quiet and reserved. Instead, try to be more assertive every chance you get. If you are talking to the checkout clerk at Starbucks, talk to her about some recent news or whatever topic that pops on your mind. You may also ask here a question. If you are at the gas station, do that with the gas attendant. If you are at an ATM and you are going into the bank, talk to the teller there.

If you're at work, and you got an opportunity to go to lunch with somebody, talk to him. Try to get yourself to talk more and be more open in those kinds of situations. Also, try to leverage every single opportunity for talking that you have throughout your day--whether it's with your kids or spouse, especially with strangers. You will find that that is where your biggest gain is going to be: with strangers.

Chapter 3 - Overcoming Shyness Effectively

One of the most common issues of introversion is shyness. This chapter will discuss tips on overcoming shyness. You will gain more practical tips that you can implement at this very moment to finally set yourself free of shyness. First, let us talk about what shyness really is.

Shyness is basically a person's tendency to feel tense, worried, or awkward during any kind of social encounters. It is especially severe during encounters with strangers. It is purely an emotional reaction. However, it does not mean it cannot manifest physical symptoms as well.

Some of the physical symptoms of shyness are sweating, pounding of the heart, blushing, and getting an upset stomach. It does not have any dangerous physical effects. However, severe cases of this trait will often prevent someone from socializing with others, preventing him from functioning in society efficiently. Therefore, shyness can be more detrimental to a person's mental, social and emotional well-being, rather than on his physical aspects.

The first thing that a person needs to remember about shyness, though, is that it is not inherent. It is only a result of the thoughts that keep running through your mind. Removing these thoughts from your mind can help you overcome this problem. Shyness is something that you acquire, either through a traumatic or embarrassing event.

If you have been suffering from this problem for a long time already, then avoid thinking that you will suffer from it your entire life. Avoid thinking that just because you're shy and introverted, you can no longer attain success.

There are many inspiring stories out there about people who were extremely introverted, but successfully acquired some vital qualities of extroverts. Their transition was so successful that if they were to intcract with you right now, you will never believe that they once have fully introverted qualities. In fact, most people who encounter them think that they are extroverts because of their exceptional socialization skills.

So how should you do it? Well first, keep in mind that shyness is something that you can definitely address and correct. You do not have to deal with it all throughout your life. Remember that the problem is only on your mind.

After changing your mindset, starts thinking of things that will help you develop a more confident demeanor. Change the way you view yourself. Get rid of the idea that people around you are always looking at you and judging your every move. One of the main reasons why there are people who suffer from severe shyness is that they think too much about what others think of them. Start removing the thought that people are always watching your every move and are waiting for the moment that you'll commit a mistake since that does not happen all the time.

In this case, it would be wise to implement the progressive desensitization process, which involves numbing yourself from the thought that how others perceive you is the most important thing in this world.

Avoid caring too much about how people see you, because if you do, you'll never be able to showcase who you truly are. You will stutter when talking to others, you won't be comfortable making eye contact, you will have a hard time introducing yourself or approaching others, and you may find it difficult to present your opinions and ideas.

Your fear of embarrassment, rejection, judgment, ridicule, and others are only constructed by your mind. There is no valid basis for such fears. Also, keep in mind that just like others, you are also normal and you have many wonderful qualities that you can share to the world.

With those things said, the best way to get rid of shyness out of your system is to go out there and interact with others. Build up your confidence to talk to people gradually. Take small steps to raising your confidence, and you will be surprised to see yourself interacting with others confidently one day.

We all know that trying not to think about the thing you are scared of is about as easy as ignoring a nasty paper cut. Instead of ignoring those thoughts, examine your fear completely. Learn how to put the reason of your shyness in context. Look at it and ask yourself, what are the odds of that actually occurring?

Know that shyness, and the fear the usually accompanies it, often comes from the right side of the brain - the emotional side. Put this fear over to the left side of your brain and take time to think logically about your situation.

Try, as much as possible, to relax. Stretch. Take long deep breaths. Keep your breathing steady and your blood pressure down. Try to release any tension you are carrying in your body. When you get scared, you often feel tensed, causing chronic pain.

It is cliché, but sometimes, the best thing to do is to face your fear and get used to it. Usually, the more often you do something, the less scary it gets. Make a decision to put yourself in the path of things that scare you, as long as these things are not dangerous of course.

Chapter 4 - How to Become More Assertive and Confident?

In this chapter, you will receive tips on raising your confidence in every facet of life. We will teach you how to handle nerve-racking situations wherever you may be.

Tip #1: Keep your N.U.T.S. Together

N.U.T.S. is an acronym for Non-negotiable Unalterable Terms. In other words, your boundaries. Each time you find yourself in an awkward position, try to ask yourself these two questions:

1. What are the things that matter to me the most in this situation?

2. What is the one thing that I refuse to compromise?

Keep in mind that your N.U.T.S. should include important priorities in life. An example of this is your health, or getting that promotion at work that you have always wanted. Either way, once you know exactly what your priorities are, it will be much easier to punch through and fight for them.

Tip #2: Be direct, honest and simple

You'd be surprised how people find someone being coy, or passive-aggressive, annoying. Remember, part of being extroverted is being upfront. If you are upfront with the people you deal with rather than being underhanded and sneaky, things will have a bigger chance of working in your favor. By doing this, you cannot only make your needs known, but also do yourself a favor.

Tip #3: Fake it Until you Make It

Do you know why many critics consider Johnny Depp as an extremely versatile actor? It's because he has the ability to assume any role and make people see the characters as they are, not the actor behind them. Johnny puts himself in the position of the character. He thinks how the character will think. He responds how he thinks the character will respond to a particular scenario.

The same thing goes with being assertive and confident. If you act it, you will start to feel like it. How do you do that? Well, just do it the way actors do. Make your presence known through your body language and your voice.

Also, do not forget to maintain good posture and speak with authority. Make assertive statements whenever appropriate. Examples of assertive statements are:

1. "Please do not sit on my chair."

2. "Why is it so noisy down there? Are you fixing something?"

3. "I know you're doing something fishy down there."

Always remember the expression, *"Do be an eagle, do not be a turtle."* Do not thrust your shoulders forward in a slump. It just makes you look like you're apologizing for yourself. Keep your back straight - stomach in, chest out. Breathe deeply and evenly. This technique will make you look more in control and engaged with the person you're talking to.

Tip #4: Make Use of "I" Statements Instead of "You" statements

When making a statement, the last thing we want to happen is sound accusatory. To avoid this, make it a point to use "I" statements, instead of "You" statements. Here is an example of a "You" statement that totally makes you sound accusatory:

"You never take out the trash. The trash bin is so full that flies are beginning to swarm to it."

Now, here is an example of an "I" statement:

"I have been the one taking out the trash since last week. I just finished double shifts at work and I am extremely exhausted. Could you take the trash out tonight?

As you can see with the "I" statement, frustrations can be expressed without looking like a nag. Remember, keep your priorities, be upfront, mind your posture, maintain eye contact, speak authoritatively, and make use of "I" statements. These things will surely bring you closer towards becoming more confident.

Chapter 5 - How to Deal with Embarrassment and Anxiety?

In this chapter, you will learn to handle embarrassment, which is also one of the progenitors of shyness and introversion, and what your brain does when you're in an embarrassing situation. We will also provide you with a 3-step technique on how to move on and brush embarrassing moments off.

Embarrassment is an inherent biological reaction, which is similar to most of the emotions that we feel every day. It occurs in the PACC, or Pregenual Anterior Cingulate Cortex, which is a boomerang-shaped area of the brain right behind the eyes.

According to UC Berkeley researchers, PACC activity is high every time a person is embarrassed. They discovered this by conducting an experiment wherein the subjects were made to sing an acapella rendition of Rick Astley's song "Never Gonna

Give You Up" and then watching their own performances on video. During this moment, each of the subject's PACC exhibited high activity and corresponded with increased heart rate, sweating foreheads and palms, and verbal expressions of awkwardness.

Embarrassment is a progenitor of low self-esteem. Low self-esteem is one probable cause of why a person is introverted. Therefore, to shed introverted tendencies and become more extroverted, we must learn how to handle embarrassment.

With that in mind, here are three tips to getting over embarrassment and boost self-confidence.

Step #1: Force Yourself not to Think that you are the Center of the Universe

Every time an embarrassing moment occurs, try to tell yourself over and over that it is not that big of a deal. Just because your mind is making it a big issue, it doesn't mean it actually is.

As a matter of fact, the "spotlight effect," which is a tried and tested scientific principle, states that people around you do not pay attention to every fault that you make at all. Another experiment that tested this principle involved students wearing bright-orange, Steve Urkel-embossed shirts to a university acquaintance party.

After the party, the students were asked how many people in the party they thought noticed the ugly shirt. Invariably, the number of people they thought noticed their ugly shirts were higher compared to actual the actual number.

Remember, before you feel so embarrassed about something, take a deep breath and repeat these words over and over in your head: "*contrary to what my brain is saying, this embarrassing moment is not a big deal.*"

Step #2: Don't Apologize, Deal With It

Apologizing excessively can be detrimental. It is not going to help you in drawing attention away from you during embarrassing situations. In fact, it's going to do the opposite. It can only draw more attention towards you.

So, instead of apologizing, try your best to downplay the moment. Apologizing too much only tells the people around you that that particular situation is a big deal, and that they should treat it as such.

Step #3: Don't Dwell, Change the Channel

Embarrassment and shame are two different things. Embarrassment is usually an instinctive and sometimes unavoidable response to an uncomfortable or delicate situation. If you fixate yourself on what happened - constantly replaying that instance over and over again in your head - that embarrassment then turns into anxiety and shame.

Believe us when we say that you do not want to carry that kind of burden with you. Instead, try to think of your mind as a television and the embarrassing moment as that boring sitcom every TV network seems to like to run. Grab the TV remote and change the channel. Replace that boring show with something uplifting--a nice moment with your special someone, a funny childhood memory, your favorite book-- or anything that will take your mind off of junk.

Remember, embarrassment is a completely healthy reaction to an awkward situation. Force yourself to remember that this is a big deal in nobody else's eyes, but your own. Do not apologize. Instead, try to downplay the moment and do replay what happened over and over again. Change the channel.

Chapter 6: Dealing with Rejection and Improve Self-Esteem

Each of us encounter some form of rejection at some point in our lives, and it hurts. Studies show that rejection is really not that far off from actual physical pain. Learning how to deal with rejection is important when it comcs to being extroverted. By learning how to cope with rejections and disappointments, you're making yourself immune to anxiety and fear that leads to shyness.

In this chapter, we're going to discuss how to deal with rejection. We are going to scrutinize why being disdained by our friends, family or peers is emotionally and psychologically damaging. Aside from that, we'll also give you three "take back your life" methods for maintaining a happy and healthy life.

If you feel angry, dismayed or even agitated after someone has rejected you, let's say a girlfriend who is not talking to you for some reason or a coworker who is totally avoiding you, it is normal. In other words, it is an inherent human reaction to feel bad every time a person is socially rejected since being part of a group or a community has so many advantages.

Humans are genetically wired to have adverse feelings when left out. It is basically how we, humans, stay alive. And do take note that we are not just talking about psychological pain, either. Let's take, for example, a study done in UCLA by neuroscientists back in 2003. These neuroscientists replicated social exclusion through a video game in which the subjects played catch with other actual human subjects.

As the game progressed, the virtual game of catch eventually became a game of monkey in the middle and the subjects who were connected to an MRI machine displayed activity in the portion of the brain that is associated with physical pain.

With that being said, science has now supported what most of us already know: it really, really feels awful to be rejected. However, as we have said before, being rejected is something that we have to deal with in life. So what are we to do? How can we prevent ourselves from feeling down every time we're rejected?

The greatest way to counteract the feeling of pain after a rejection is to take control in deciding how to respond to it. This brings us to the 3-step method in taking back your life.

Step #1: Beef up your Self-esteem

Many studies show that when excluded from a social group, individuals who exhibit low self-esteem can sink into, depression, physical sickness and a whole lot of other maladies. A solution to this is to develop and raise your self-esteem now.

We do know that this is easier said than done. Staying away from irrational and negative thoughts is like keeping the bees away from the honey. However, try to think things through in a logical, instead of emotional, manner. On a piece of paper, jot down three of your biggest accomplishments in life.

Our goal here is to not define your whole individuality with just one traumatic event. Instead, aim to define your true self with your accomplishments - your life experiences. Look at the list that you made, know your true worth and believe in who you really are. Take note that accomplishments are not easily achievable. Believe us when we say that you can soar right above all these negativities.

Step #2: Treat your Injuries

Whatever emotional pain you are, feeling right now is indiscernible from physical pain in your brain. So, why not treat it as actual physical pain as well? Think of it as being in the recovery stage. Psychiatrists say that it is essential to keep an excellent physical health during times of emotional distress.

Try to get more hours of sleep at night. Take your meals on time and stick to a much healthier diet, preferably more veggies and fruits. Try to exercise at least half an hour a day. This will facilitate the release of endorphins in your brain, thereby facilitating a sense of well-being. Your removal peak will stay high if you keep yourself in a much healthier state.

Step #3: Get Proactive

Think of this as a great opportunity to make new friends that you have more in common with. Look for youth groups, social clubs and team sports. Join a new social circle and pursue things that pique your interests. Use an excuse to practice that newfound self-confidence and really go out to meet new people. Odds are you'll find a group of friends with whom you will fit right in.

So remember, by taking control of your life, a control you thought you lost when you were socially rejected, you're less likely be emotionally bogged down by what happened. You can do that by taking care of yourself physically, working to raise your self-esteem, and reaching out to form new friend groups.

Chapter 7 - Making Real World Social Improvements

Therefore, you are looking for better ways on how to be more social right now - becoming a solid extrovert. If you are searching online for tips on how to do it, you may find people talking about going out there and practicing. These types of tips, however, are illogical. Why? Because in the real world, you can't just go up to somebody and talk about your passion, how your day has been, your lifelong dreams, and so forth. You run the risk of embarrassment, or worse, making a fool out of yourself.

So you may be wondering, how do you practice your social skills without actually going out there and embarrassing yourself? Well, we'll try to find the answer to this question by first answering this question: When you want to be good at something, do you set a main goal for yourself that will take huge amounts of motivation and will take years to accomplish, or do you set small achievable goals that will serve as stepping stones to achieve your main goal?

If you want to get lean and healthy, for example, do you set a goal of waking up two hours earlier than usual and go out for a 2-hour run 6 days a week? Of course not. You're going to get burned up. You see, a better approach for getting healthier and leaner is to just set a goal of waking up 15 minutes earlier and go for a 15-minute walk around the block.

The beauty of this is that you can make a habit out of it quickly. It will not put your body under undue stress by doing something drastically intensive all of a sudden. This is also the reason why fitness instructors remind people to stretch before working out.

Once you develop the habit of waking up 15 minutes earlier than usual, you can build on top of that. You can wake up 25 minutes earlier this time and do a quick 20-minute jog around the block, instead of just the usual walk. Once you're used to that, you can raise the bar again for the next goal. In other words, you can stretch your initial set of goals further and further until you reach your main goal.

The same goes for your social skills. Instead of creating a huge goal right off the bat and motivating yourself really hard to achieve it, you want to just set a small goal - something that is achievable and you can do over and over again without any conscious motivation. Once you achieve that and make it into a habit, you can begin to build on top of it.

At this point you may be wondering, what kind of set goals are we talking about here? Well, it can be as simple as saying "Hi" to the person at the reception desk at the office, or saying a simple "Hello" to the cashier every time you check out of the local grocery store. If you do this for a couple of weeks, you can develop it into a habit. It will be easier for you to achieve this small goal, then.

The next level up could be asking the cashier how her day is going, instead of the usual "Hello." If you create this ritual and make it into a habit, it is going to become effortless. So again, instead of setting an extremely big goal for your social skills right away, like starting a huge intellectual conversation or making a big group of people laugh, you want to make small commitments first. You want to set small, achievable goals and do them repeatedly so they become a habit. From there, you can raise the bar on those goals until you get to your main goal.

Chapter 8 - How to Constantly Improve Socially?

Some of you may be reading this book because some sort of event happened recently that made you realize your social skills really suck. You may have also browsed online and found tips on how to become a bonafide extrovert. If you actually tried the tips you found online - from a blog post or webpage – you may have realized that you will improve just a little. And, after a while, you will revert back to you old self. You start to lose that skill or hit a plateau and stop improving.

The real question in this case then is, how do you keep on improving? Well, try doing this: Choose 5 or 6 friends closest to you and look at their health, their finance, their level of education, and so forth. After that, think about their level of social skills. Do they have the same level of health, finance, education and social skills as you? Chances are, they do not.

The point is, you need to be mindful of the kind of people you surround yourself with. If you're surrounded by positive people, you can definitely improve on everything that you do. If you're surrounded by negative people, you're definitely on your way to a very bad place; it's not somewhere you want to go.

So, what you want to do is identify the people around you with high social skills, and you want to spend as much time with them as possible. If you surround yourself with social butterflies, or people with high social skills, then you are going to pick up on all of their social traits and improve automatically. By doing so, you can begin to improve on your social skills without even trying.

Conclusion

Overcoming shyness and being confident can take some getting used to. However, it is not as hard as some people say it is. Practice is the key to success and we urge each and every one of you who is reading this book to implement every point that we discussed.

We thank you for purchasing this book, *Extrovert Yourself: How to Become Extrovert, Confident and Overcome Shyness.* We hope that we have imparted great tips and techniques for you to overcome your introverted tendencies and make living in an extroverted world much, much easier.

From this point onward, we encourage you to set achievement milestones for each chapter that you successfully implement in your life. With the guidance from this book and constant practice, you are well on your way to becoming an extroverted individual.

Finally, if you enjoyed this book, then I'd like to ask you for a favor, would you be kind enough to leave a review for this book on Amazon? It'd be greatly appreciated!

Thank you and good luck!

27437678R00031

Printed in Great Britain
by Amazon